A Kid's Guide to Drawing™

How to Draw
Dinosaurs

Laura Murawski™

The Rosen Publishing Group's
PowerKids Press™
New York

Published in 2001 by The Rosen Publishing Group, Inc.
29 East 21st Street, New York, NY 10010

First Edition

Book Design: Kim Sonsky

Illustration Credits: Laura Murawski

Photo Credits: Title page (hand) by Arlan Dean; pp. 6, 12, 14 © Joe Tucciarone/Science Photo Library; p. 8 courtesy Department of Library Services/American Museum of Natural History; p. 10 © Carlyn Iverson/Photo Researchers, Inc.; p. 16 courtesy of Independent Photo Researchers; p. 18 © Chris Butler/Science Photo Library; p. 21 © SuperStock.

Murawski, Laura.
    How to draw dinosaurs/ Laura Murawski.—1st ed.
      p. cm.— (A kid's guide to drawing)
    Includes index.
    Summary: Describes how to draw various dinosaurs, including the stegosaurus, camarasaurus, and T-Rex.
    ISBN 0-8239-5550-8 (alk. paper)
    1. Dinosaurs in art—Juvenile literature. 2. Drawing—Technique—Juvenile literature.
  [1. Dinosaurs in art. 2. Drawing—Technique.] I. Title.
  NC780.5. M865 2000
  743.6—dc21   00-028046

Manufactured in the United States of America

CONTENTS

Let's Draw Dinosaurs

Drawing dinosaurs is exciting and easy! Do you like dinosaurs? Do you find them interesting but perhaps a little bit scary? They might look terrifying but they are not terrifying to draw! Just follow the step-by-step instructions under each drawing and you'll be creating a fierce *Tyrannosaurus rex* in no time!

You'll learn about many kinds of dinosaurs and when they lived. Dinosaurs existed during the **Mesozoic era**. This era is divided into three periods: the Triassic (250–205 million years ago), the Jurassic (205–144 million years ago), and the Cretaceous (144–66 million years ago). In this book, you will learn about eight dinosaurs from the Mesozoic era, and how to draw them.

Here's a list of the supplies you will need for drawing:

- A sketch pad
- A number 2 pencil
- A pencil sharpener
- An eraser

4

To draw dinosaurs, you will begin by making one simple shape and then you will add other shapes to it. The basic shapes you use to draw dinosaurs are <u>ovals</u>, <u>circles</u>, and <u>curved lines</u>. Some of these drawing terms might be new to you. In the section of this book called Drawing Terms, on page 22, you can find these words with illustrations to show what they look like.

The first drawing you will learn about is *Stegosaurus*. You'll be able to draw *Stegosaurus* in six steps! All the dinosaur drawings begin with an oval and then have circles added to the oval. There are directions under each drawing to help you through the step. Each new step is shown in color to help guide you.

To draw dinosaurs, use the four Ps: **Patience**, **Persistence**, Practice, and a Positive **attitude**. With a little practice, the drawings will get easier. Before you start, try to find a quiet, clean, and well-lit space where you can pay attention to your drawing. Good luck, and most important, have fun! Now sharpen your pencils, and let's begin drawing!

Stegosaurus

Stegosaurus lived during the Late Jurassic period more than 140 million years ago. Even though this dinosaur was about as tall as an elephant, its brain was only the size of a walnut. Stegosaurus was not a very smart dinosaur. It was an unusual looking dinosaur, though. Its name means "plated lizard" in Greek. Plates ran down its neck and back, and it had spikes on its tail. The plates were made of bone, but they were hollow with tubelike tunnels inside. Some scientists say that the plates helped Stegosaurus warm up and cool down its body. Each of its tail spikes was about 3 feet (0.9 m) long. These were used to protect it during fights with **predators**. Stegosaurus was a **herbivore**, which means it only ate plants.

1

Begin by drawing a large beanlike shape to make the body of *Stegosaurus*.

4

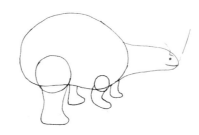

Draw the neck and the head by adding a curved shape onto the right side of the body. Add a dot for the eye and a line for the mouth.

2

Next, draw two <u>circles</u> at the bottom of the beanlike shape to begin drawing the legs. Notice where they are placed and that one circle is larger than the other.

5

Now draw the tail by making two long, <u>curved lines</u> from the back, or left, of the body. Make the two lines come to a point. This is the end of the tail. Draw four pointed shapes near the end of the tail for the spikes.

3

Now draw all four legs by using the shapes shown.

6

Erase the extra lines on the body. Next, draw a set of <u>triangles</u> and a set of <u>diamond</u> shapes on the top, or back, of the body, to make the plates. Notice how the set of triangles runs along the top line of the body. The diamonds join the points of the triangles. You're done!

Camarasaurus

    Camarasaurus was a **sauropod**. Sauropods were huge plant-eating dinosaurs with long necks and small heads. *Camarasaurus* weighed 20 tons (18 tonnes) and measured about 60 feet (18 m) long from head to tail. *Camarasaurus* means "chambered lizard" in Greek. Its backbone had hollow chambers to lighten its weight. Compared to other sauropods the *Camarasaurus* was small. *Brachiosaurus*, for example, was 75 feet (23 m) long. *Camarasaurus* was a herbivore and had spoon-shaped teeth. It ate whole leaves without chewing them. To help with digestion, *Camarasaurus* had **gizzard stones** in its stomach. *Camarasaurus* lived during the Late Jurassic period, 155 million years ago.

1

Begin by drawing a large <u>oval</u> to make the body of *Camarasaurus*.

2

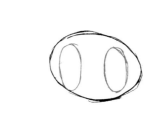

Next, draw two ovals inside the first oval to begin drawing the legs. Notice where they are placed inside the large oval. Then draw another oval outside the largest oval to the upper left. This smaller oval is the head.

3

Draw two small circles at the bottom of the ovals. Finish the legs by drawing two <u>rectangles</u> under the small circles.

4

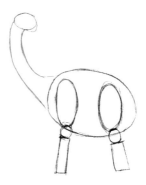

Draw the neck by connecting the upper left oval to the body with two curved lines.

5

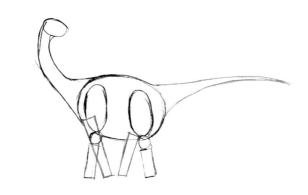

Now draw the other two legs by making two more rectangles coming from the large ovals. Draw the tail by making two long, curved lines coming out from the right side of the body. The two lines should come to a point at the end.

6

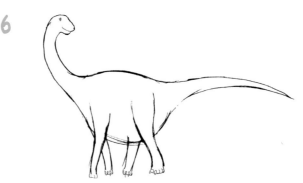

Clean up the legs by connecting the shapes with curved lines. Erase any extra lines. Finish the face by drawing a line for the mouth and a dot for the eye. Add curved lines to the feet.
That's it! You're done!

Tyrannosaurus rex

Tyrannosaurus rex or T. rex was a very powerful dinosaur. Its name means "**tyrant** lizard king" in Greek. T. rex walked on two strong hind legs. Its head was so big that its skull alone measured 4 feet (1.2 m) long! Its teeth were about nine inches (22.9 cm) long! T. rex took big bites out of its **prey** and then ate it. T. rex was not the largest dinosaur. It was only about 47 feet (14 m) long and weighed almost 8 tons (7.2 tonnes). T. rex lived over 85 million years ago during the Cretaceous period. It was one of the last to **evolve** before dinosaurs became **extinct**. One belief about why dinosaurs became extinct is that an **asteroid** from space hit Earth and caused major changes in the **climate**. Dinosaurs were not able to **adapt**, and soon died.

1

Begin by drawing a large oval to make the body shape of the *Tyrannosaurus rex*.

2

Next, draw a smaller, tilted oval to the upper right of the large oval. This smaller oval is the head.

3

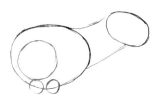

Join the ovals with two curved lines to make the neck. Add a circle inside and off center of the large oval. Draw two small circles under the large circle to begin the legs.

4

Draw two rectangles coming from the small circles. Draw the feet by making two <u>angular shapes</u> beneath the rectangles.

5

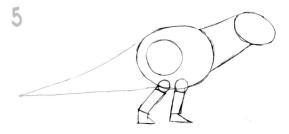

Now draw two long lines out from the back of the body. Make sure the lines come to a point. Excellent! You just made the tail!

6

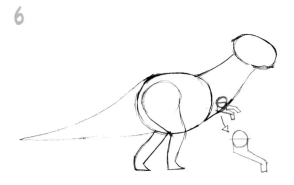

Clean up the lines of the legs by joining the shapes with curved lines and erasing any extra lines. Draw the tiny arms by first drawing a circle. Then draw the shape below the circle as shown.

7

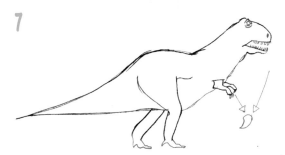

Erase any extra lines. Finish the face by drawing an open mouth, teeth, an eye, and a nostril. Add details to the feet and hands as shown. Great job! You just drew the fierce *T. rex*!

Velociraptor

Velociraptor was one of the fastest dinosaurs. Its name in Latin means "swift robber" because it could run up to 40 miles (64 km) per hour and it had clawed hands that it used to grab things! Velociraptor's small body helped it move fast. It was only about 6 feet (1.8 m) long and 3 feet (0.9 m) tall. It weighed between 15 and 33 pounds (7 and 15 kg). Velociraptor was so small that it had to hunt in packs to survive. One of its greatest weapons was its 7-inch (18-cm) claw on its middle toe. Velociraptor was a **carnivore**, which means it ate meat. It was one of the smartest dinosaurs. Scientists think this because Velociraptor's body was very small but its brain was very big. It lived in the Cretaceous period, about 85 million years ago.

1

Begin by drawing a large oval to make the body of *Velociraptor*.

2

Next, draw four small circles. Notice their different sizes and where they are placed inside and outside of the oval.

3

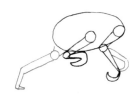

Now join the circles with lines to make one front leg and one back leg. Make the feet look like hooks as shown.

4

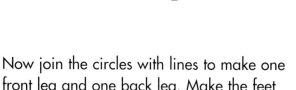

Add the second front, hooklike leg. Draw another circle for the second back leg, which will be stretched out. Finish the back leg by drawing in the shapes as shown.

5

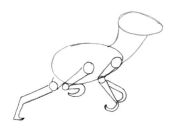

Next, draw an oval to the upper-right of the body for the head. Draw the neck by making two curved lines from the head to the body.

6

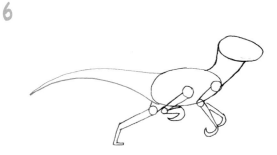

Next, add the tail. Draw two lines out from the back of the body. Notice how these lines end in a point.

7

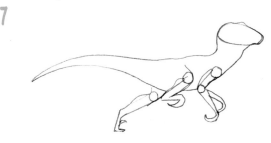

Begin to shape the dinosaur by curving the lines of the legs, body, and head as shown.

8

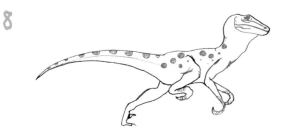

Erase any extra lines. Draw the eyes, mouth, and nose. Add circles to the body and tail and fill them in.

Deinonychus

Deinonychus was graceful and fast like a bird. It was also very smart. It measured between 8 and 13 feet (2.4 and 4 m) long and 5 feet (1.5 m) tall. It weighed up to 175 pounds (75 kg). *Deinonychus* means "terrible claw" in Greek. It had big curved claws for its fingers and toes. On the second toe of each foot it had a 5-inch (12.7-cm) curved claw. It used its claws to tear open the bellies of its prey. The combination of its size, speed, cleverness, and claws made *Deinonychus* very dangerous. *Deinonychus* was a carnivore. It lived during the Cretaceous period, about 144 to 97 million years ago.

1

Begin by drawing a large oval to make the body of *Deinonychus*.

2

Draw two smaller, thinner ovals to start the legs. Tilt them as shown. Draw the larger oval at the left, over and across the body oval.

3

Now draw five small circles to continue drawing the legs.

4

Draw lines connecting the circles to complete the legs. Then add angular shapes for the feet and hands.

5

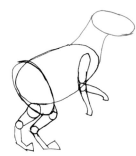

Next, draw an oval above and to the right of the body for the head. Join this oval to the body with two curved lines.

6

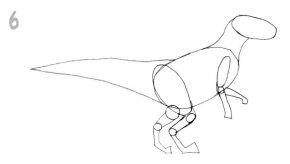

Now draw the tail by making two long, curved lines from the back of the body. Notice how these lines come to a point at the end.

7

Add the eye, nose, and mouth to the face. Add claws to the hands and feet as shown. Make the center claws on the back feet longer.

8

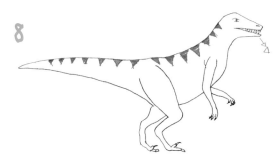

Erase extra lines. Add teeth and upside-down triangles along the back and shade them.

Maiasaura

Maiasaura means "good mother lizard" in Greek. **Fossils** of adult and young Maiasaura were found in nests in Montana. This find was very exciting for scientists. It proved that Maiasaura lived in **colonies** and cared for its young. Dinosaur mothers usually did not take care of their babies. They laid eggs and then abandoned them. Maiasaura was about 30 feet (9 m) long and 8 feet (2.4 m) tall. It weighed about 3 tons (2.7 tonnes). It had a ducklike bill. Maiasaura was a herbivore and could eat about 200 pounds (91 kg) of plants each day! It walked mostly on its hind legs but it could use all four when it needed to move quickly. This dinosaur lived during the Cretaceous period, about 80 million years ago.

1

Begin by drawing a large oval to make the body of *Maiasaura*.

2

Next, draw five circles. Notice their different sizes and where they are placed inside and outside of the oval.

3

Now connect the circles with lines to make one front leg and one back leg.

4

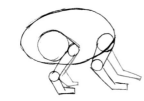

Draw the other back and front legs as shown by making similar shapes to the ones you drew in Step 3.

5

Draw an oval to the upper-right of the body for the head. Add the neck by drawing two curved lines, joining the head to the body.

6

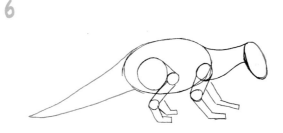

Next, add the tail. Draw two lines at the left of the large oval of the body. Make these lines come to a point at the end.

7

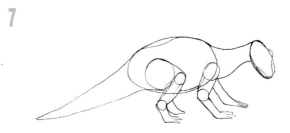

Now begin to shape the dinosaur. Curve the lines in the legs, body, and head as shown. Draw in the feet, and make the toes pointed.

8

Erase any extra lines. Draw the eyes, nose, and mouth. Add a thick stripe along the back and fill it in.

Brachiosaurus

   Brachiosaurus is the largest dinosaur for which scientists have found a complete skeleton. It lived during the Late Jurassic period, about 140 million years ago. The *Brachiosaurus* was about 75 feet (23 m) long and 41 feet (12.6 m) tall. It had one of the longest necks of all dinosaurs. It weighed about 89 tons (80 tonnes). This dinosaur's long neck allowed it to reach the tops of trees to eat leaves that many other dinosaurs were unable to reach. *Brachiosaaurus* was a herbivore. It also had front legs that were longer than its back legs, just like today's giraffe's. *Brachio* means "arm" in Latin and *saurus* means "lizard" in Greek. Its name probably referred to its long neck that could reach to the treetops. It had a tiny, deep, and domed head with a wide, flat nose.

1

Begin by drawing a large oval to make the body of *Brachiosaurus*.

2

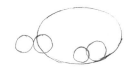

Next, draw four small circles for the legs. Notice where the circles are placed inside and outside the oval.

3

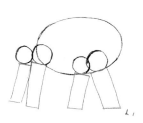

Now draw four tilted rectangles below the circles.

4

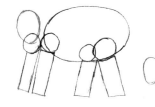

Draw two more small ovals. Place one so it goes through the circle farthest to the left. Draw the other oval over to the lower right, away from the rectangles.

5

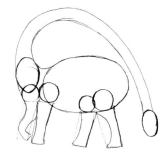

Join these two ovals by drawing two curved lines for the long neck. Draw in the legs by curving the lines of the rectangles.

6

Clean up the legs by erasing part of the circles. Erase any extra lines. Draw lines inside the neck as shown.

7

Add the tail by drawing two curved lines out from the back of the body that end in a point.

8

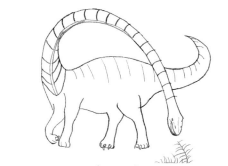

Draw an eye, mouth, and nose. Add toes to the feet as shown. Add lines to the front, back, and tail.

19

Styracosaurus

Styracosaurus means "spiked lizard" in Greek. It was a strange-looking horned dinosaur. It had at least nine spikes on its head! It had one large horn growing on its nose that was 2 feet (61 cm) long and 6 inches (15 cm) wide. There were two smaller horns above its eyes and six spikes that pointed up and back, over its neck. There were also smaller spikes and bumps along the edges of its neck. These horns and spikes helped protect *Styracosaurus* during fights. *Styracosaurus* walked on four legs and weighed up to 3 tons (2.8 tonnes)! This dinosaur lived about 70 million years ago during the Cretaceous period.

1

Begin by drawing a large oval to make the body of *Styracosaurus*.

2

Next, draw four circles. Notice their different sizes and where they are placed in the oval.

3

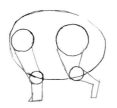

Now connect the circles with lines to make a front leg, back leg, and two feet.

4

Draw a circle for the other front leg and add lines to finish it. Draw another back leg by making the angular shape as shown.

5

Now draw an oval for the head. Draw two curved lines to connect the head to the body.

6

Add a <u>teardrop shape</u> near the top of the head. At the right of the oval, add two curved lines that meet at a point for the tail.

7

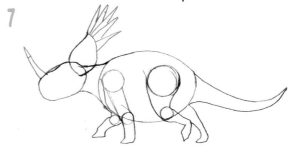

Draw a pointy horn and spikes on the nose and head. Add a line for the front leg.

8

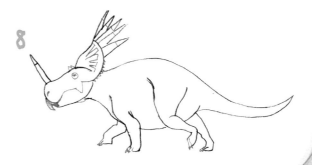

Erase extra lines. Draw the eyes, nose, upper face, and feet as shown.

Drawing Terms

Words and shapes used to draw dinosaurs include the following:

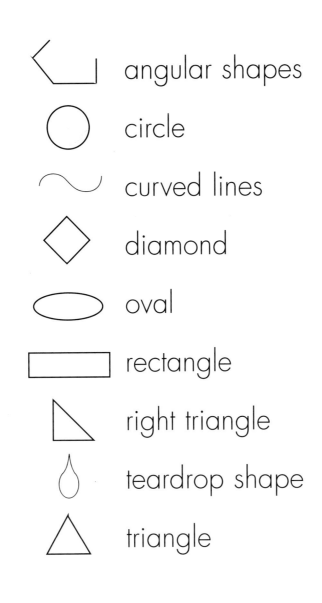

angular shapes

circle

curved lines

diamond

oval

rectangle

right triangle

teardrop shape

triangle

Glossary

adapt (uh-DAPT) To change to fit new conditions.

asteroid (as-tehr-OYD) A small planet in space that revolves around the sun.

attitude (AH-tih-tood) A way of thinking, acting, or feeling.

carnivore (KAR-nih-vor) An animal that eats other animals for food.

climate (KLY-mit) The kind of weather in a certain area.

colonies (KAH-luh-neez) Groups of living things of the same kind that grow and live together.

evolve (ee-VOLV) To develop and change over many, many years.

extinct (ik-STINKT) To no longer exist.

fossils (FAH-sulz) The hardened remains of a dead animal or plant that lived long ago.

gizzard stones (GIH-zurd STONZ) Part of the stomach that helps grind up food.

herbivore (HER-beh-vor) An animal that eats plants.

Mesozoic era (meh-zeh-ZOH-ik IR-eh) A period of history when birds and animals first lived on Earth. It includes three periods, Cretaceous, Jurassic, and Triassic.

patience (PAY-shunts) The ability to wait calmly for something.

persistence (pur-SIS-tehns) The act of continuing something or refusing to stop doing something.

predators (PREH-duh-ters) Animals that kill other animals for food.

prey (PRAY) An animal that is hunted by another animal for food.

sauropod (SOR-uh-pahd) Any of a group of large four-footed, plant-eating dinosaurs with long necks and tails and small heads.

tyrant (TY-rint) A mean ruler.

Index

Web Sites

Due to the changing nature of Internet links, PowerKids Press has developed an online list of Web sites related to the subject of this book. This site is updated regularly. Please use this link to access the list:
www.powerkidslinks.com/kgd/dinosaurs/